OUR BODIES

REPRODUCTION

Steve Parker

WAYLAND

Titles in the series:
The Brain and Nervous System • Digestion
The Heart, Lungs and Blood • Reproduction
The Senses • The Skeleton and Muscles

Produced by Monkey Puzzle Media Ltd
Gissing's Farm, Fressingfield, Suffolk IP21 5SH, UK

Text copyright © 2004 Steve Parker
Series copyright © 2004 Wayland
First published in 2004 by Hodder Wayland
an imprint of Hodder Children's Books

This paperback edition published in 2007 by Wayland,
an imprint of Hachette Children's Books

Commissioning Editor: Victoria Brooker
Book Editor: Nicola Edwards
Design: Jane Hawkins
Picture Research: Sally Cole
Artwork: Peter Bull
Consultant: Dr Trish Groves

British Library Cataloguing in Publication Data
Parker, Steve, 1952–
 Reproduction – (Our bodies)
 1. Human reproduction – Juvenile literature
 I.Title
 612.6

 ISBN – 13: 978 0 7502 3725 3

Printed and bound in China

Wayland,
an imprint of Hachette Children's Books
338 Euston Road, London NW1 3BH

Picture Acknowledgements
Alamy 7, 28, 32, 40, 43 top; Ardea 25 (John Cancalosi); Corbis 4 (Walter Hodges), 27 (Laura
Doss), 36 (Ariel Skelley), 44 (Tom Stewart); Digital Vision 13; FLPA 35 bottom (Eddie Schuiling);
Nature Picture Library 45 (Peter Oxford); Science Photo Library *front cover* inset (CNRI), 9 (Dr
Yorgos Nikas), 11 (John Burbidge), 15 top (CNRI), 17 (Prof P Motta/Department of Anatomy,
Univ. La Sapienza, Rome), 16 (D Philips), 19 (Andy Walker, Midland Fertility Services), 21 (Hank
Morgan), 23 (Alexander Tsiaras), 29 (Astrid & Hanns-Frieder Michler), 31 left (SIU School of
Medicine), 31 right (Stephen J Krasemann), 33 (BSIP Astier), 35 top (John Cole), 39 (Saturn
Stills), 41 (Andy Levin); Still Pictures 5 (J Alcalay and B Marcon); Topham Picturepoint 1
(ImageWorks), 37 (Image Works).

CONTENTS

INTRODUCTION   4

FEMALE REPRODUCTIVE ORGANS   6

THE FEMALE CYCLE   8
EGG PRODUCTION   10

MALE REPRODUCTIVE ORGANS   12

SPERM PRODUCTION   14

THE REPRODUCTIVE PROCESS   16

THE FIRST WEEK   18
REPRODUCTIVE PROBLEMS (FOCUS ON HEALTH)   20
THE EARLY EMBRYO   22
GROWTH IN THE WOMB   24
LIFE SUPPORT IN THE WOMB   26
TOWARDS BIRTH   28
THE DAY OF BIRTH (CASE STUDY)   30
A NEW BABY   32
BIRTH PROBLEMS (FOCUS ON HEALTH)   34

GROWING UP   36

THE YOUNG CHILD   38
THE OLDER CHILD   40
CHILD TO ADULT   42
THE NEXT GENERATION (CASE STUDY)   44

GLOSSARY   46
FURTHER INFORMATION   47
INDEX   48

INTRODUCTION

A vital process

Reproduction is a vital feature of life. It means that living things make or produce more of their own kind – they 'have babies'. All forms of life reproduce, including plants and animals and microbes, from the tiniest germs and worms to gigantic whales and redwood trees. Each living thing has special parts which work together to reproduce or breed. These parts are known as the reproductive system.

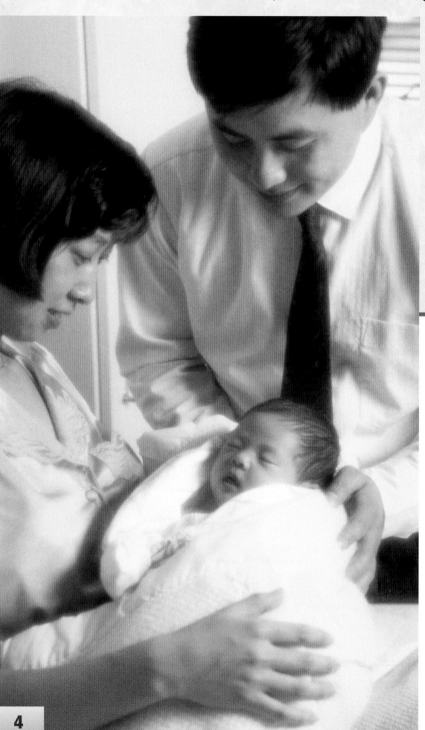

The start of a new life – not for the baby, which has already been developing for nine months, but for the parents. They now have a new family member who will drastically change their daily routine.

STAGES OF REPRODUCTION

The main parts of the reproductive system, and the way they work, are similar in a huge range of animals and in humans, too. The process of reproduction happens in several stages. A female and male get together and mate or have sex (sexual intercourse). Inside the female's body, a tiny sperm cell from the male joins or fertilizes a tiny egg cell from the female to make a fertilized egg. The fertilized egg cell, which is smaller than the dot on this letter i, multiplies and starts to form a baby which grows over weeks and months inside the mother's body – this is the time of pregnancy. After the baby is born it continues to grow bigger and stronger over weeks, months and years. Gradually it becomes a mature adult, able to reproduce.

VIEWS ABOUT REPRODUCTION

The ways that people describe human reproduction, and their views about sex, pregnancy, birth and growing up, vary hugely around the world. These views and attitudes are often based on culture and tradition, or even on modern science. They can differ from one nation to another, and between various faiths and ethnic groups, and also among people of different ages and backgrounds – even among different members of a family.

A baby orang-utan receives devoted care and attention from its mother for three years or more. Among animals, the mammals called primates – monkeys and apes – have long periods of parental care.

FEMALE REPRODUCTIVE ORGANS

Female system

There are many sizes, shapes and ages of human bodies, from small to large, thin to wide, young to old. But each is either one sex or the other – female or male, depending on its reproductive parts. The main parts of the female reproductive system, also called the sex organs, are the ovaries, oviducts (fallopian tubes), uterus (womb), cervix and vagina.

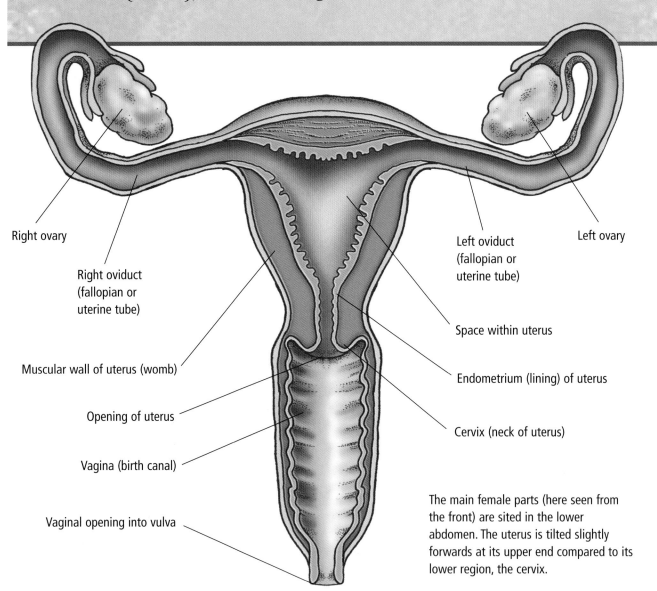

Right ovary

Right oviduct (fallopian or uterine tube)

Muscular wall of uterus (womb)

Opening of uterus

Vagina (birth canal)

Vaginal opening into vulva

Left oviduct (fallopian or uterine tube)

Left ovary

Space within uterus

Endometrium (lining) of uterus

Cervix (neck of uterus)

The main female parts (here seen from the front) are sited in the lower abdomen. The uterus is tilted slightly forwards at its upper end compared to its lower region, the cervix.

OVARIES

Each of the two ovaries is a slightly flattened egg shape, slightly smaller than a thumb, and sited in the side of the lower abdomen, just below the level of the navel ('belly-button'). About once every four weeks, one of the ovaries releases a tiny egg cell for the reproductive process, as shown on page 10.

OVIDUCTS AND UTERUS

The released egg cell passes into the oviduct, also called the fallopian tube, egg tube or uterine tube. This is about 10 centimetres long and carries the egg towards the uterus (womb). The womb is about the size and shape of an upside-down pear, tilted forwards in the base of the abdomen. If the egg cell is joined by a sperm cell, it starts to grow and develop into a baby inside the uterus.

CERVIX AND BIRTH CANAL

The rearmost, lower, narrow 'neck' of the uterus is called the cervix. Its opening leads into the vagina, or birth canal, which is about 8–9 centimetres long and opens to the outside of the body at the lower front, between the legs. When a baby is born it passes out of the uterus, through the cervical opening and along the vagina, to the outside. The outer part of the vagina is called the vulva.

weblinks

To find out more about the female reproductive organs, go to: www.waylinks.co.uk/series/ourbodies/reproduction

ANIMAL VERSUS HUMAN

A human baby develops inside its mother for nine months. This time is called pregnancy or gestation. Animals which are similar in size to humans have similar gestation times. In small creatures like mice the gestation time is much shorter, 2–3 weeks. In the largest land animal, the elephant, it is 22 months.

A mother elephant is about to give birth after a pregnancy of almost two years. The new baby will weigh about 100 kilograms – that's 30 times heavier than a human baby.

THE FEMALE CYCLE

A four-week process

For an egg cell to join with a sperm cell, it must be released from its ovary. This is called ovulation and it usually takes place about once every four weeks. Also it usually happens in alternate ovaries – first the left, then the right ovary, then the left, and so on. The four-week process of egg ripening and release, and preparation of the uterus for the baby, is called the female cycle or menstrual cycle.

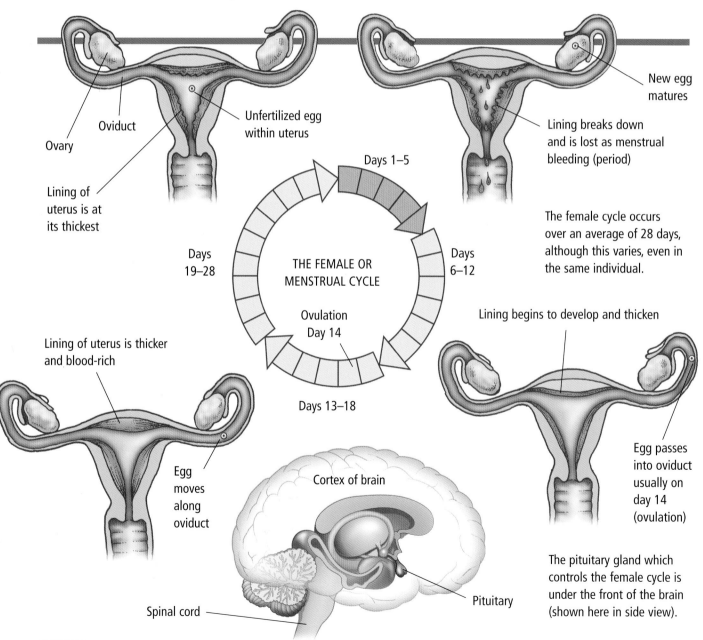

Oviduct

Ovary

Unfertilized egg within uterus

Lining of uterus is at its thickest

New egg matures

Lining breaks down and is lost as menstrual bleeding (period)

Days 19–28

Days 1–5

THE FEMALE OR MENSTRUAL CYCLE

Ovulation Day 14

Days 6–12

The female cycle occurs over an average of 28 days, although this varies, even in the same individual.

Days 13–18

Lining begins to develop and thicken

Lining of uterus is thicker and blood-rich

Egg moves along oviduct

Cortex of brain

Egg passes into oviduct usually on day 14 (ovulation)

Spinal cord

Pituitary

The pituitary gland which controls the female cycle is under the front of the brain (shown here in side view).

HORMONES

The cycle is controlled by four natural body chemicals or hormones – oestrogen, follicle stimulating hormone (FSH), luteinizing hormone (LH) and progesterone. Oestrogen is the main female hormone, made in the ovaries. At the start of the cycle oestrogen makes one of the egg cells begin to ripen, inside a tiny fluid-filled container or follicle within the ovary (see next page). Oestrogen also makes the inner lining of the uterus thicken with blood-rich tissues, preparing it to receive the fertilized egg (see panel). The next hormone, FSH, is made in the pituitary gland just under the front of the brain. It travels in the blood to the ovary and causes the follicle to grow larger and the egg to ripen further.

OVULATION

Next LH, also from the pituitary gland, causes the egg to be released or ovulated, ready for fertilization. This usually happens halfway through the cycle. Then the empty follicle still in the ovary makes a fourth hormone, progesterone. This keeps the inner lining of the uterus thick and blood-rich, ready to nourish the egg cell if it has joined with a sperm cell. If the egg and sperm do not join, the thickened lining of the uterus isn't needed, so it breaks down. With the egg it is lost through the cervix and vagina, as the menstrual

MICRO-BODY

The uterine lining is called the endometrium. In the first phase of the female cycle it becomes much thicker and filled with extra blood vessels, under the control of oestrogen. In the second phase it stays thickened and blood-rich, under the control of progesterone.

Microscopic cells of many kinds multiply in the uterus lining, at about day 10 of the cycle.

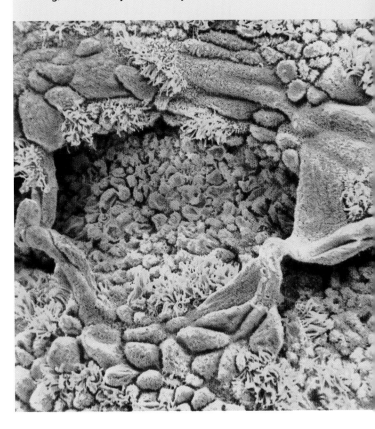

blood flow or period. Each period usually lasts 4–7 days and, on average, 60 millilitres of blood are lost in total each month. The first day of the period is counted as day one of the next female cycle, and the whole process begins again. Periods usually start between the ages of 11–16 and stop between 45–55.

EGG PRODUCTION

The eggs ripen

At the beginning of each female cycle, about 15–20 egg cells begin to ripen in one of the ovaries. Each egg is in a tiny bag-like container, the follicle, and each follicle enlarges as it fills with fluid. The batch of follicles is just under the outer covering of the ovary, known as the germinal epithelium. As the follicles fill with fluid and enlarge, they move deeper into the underlying part of the ovary, which is called the medulla.

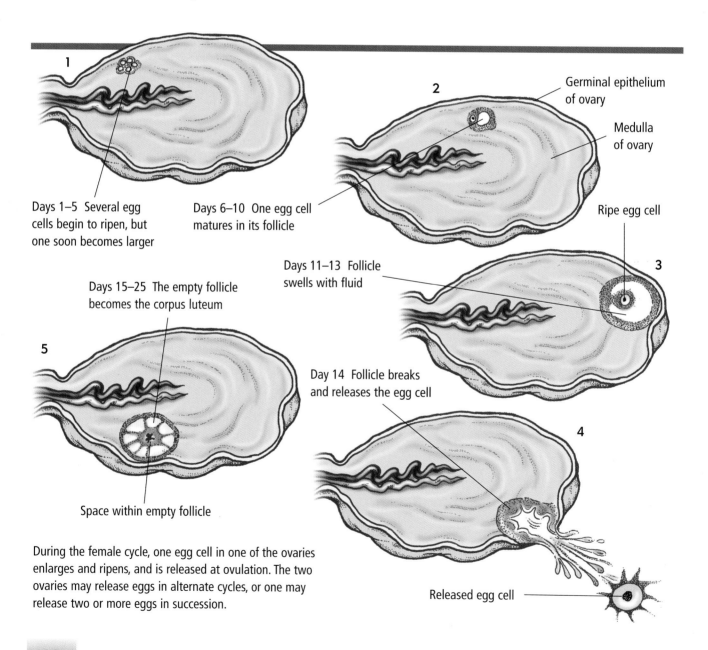

1

Days 1–5 Several egg cells begin to ripen, but one soon becomes larger

Days 6–10 One egg cell matures in its follicle

2

Germinal epithelium of ovary

Medulla of ovary

Ripe egg cell

Days 11–13 Follicle swells with fluid

3

Days 15–25 The empty follicle becomes the corpus luteum

5

Space within empty follicle

Day 14 Follicle breaks and releases the egg cell

4

Released egg cell

During the female cycle, one egg cell in one of the ovaries enlarges and ripens, and is released at ovulation. The two ovaries may release eggs in alternate cycles, or one may release two or more eggs in succession.

OVULATION

Usually only one egg cell, from the batch that begins to develop, reaches the final stage of ripening each month. Its follicle enlarges to several millimetres across and moves outwards from the medulla of the ovary, to form a small bulge at the ovary's surface. Under the influence of luteinizing hormone, the follicle breaks or ruptures and releases its fluid and the egg cell, which is now about one-tenth of one millimetre across. This stage is called ovulation. The released egg cell then passes into the funnel-shaped opening of the oviduct, which is very close to the ovary. If the egg joins a sperm cell, this usually happens in the oviduct (see page 17).

AFTER OVULATION

The egg cell leaves behind an empty follicle in the ovary. This becomes thickened and filled with a yellowish material that makes hormones, especially oestrogen and progesterone. It is about 10 millimetres across and known as the corpus luteum or 'yellow body'.

— **weblinks** —

To find out more about egg production, go to:
www.waylinks.co.uk/series/ourbodies/reproduction

MICRO-BODY

The fully ripe egg cell sits within fluid in its bubble-like follicle. The egg cell is surrounded by a mass of other microscopic cells. These other cells look tiny compared to the egg, but in fact, they are the normal size for body cells – the egg itself is relatively huge.

The fluid-filled ripe follicle (large pink area) dominates the ovary, with the egg cell in its lower left part.

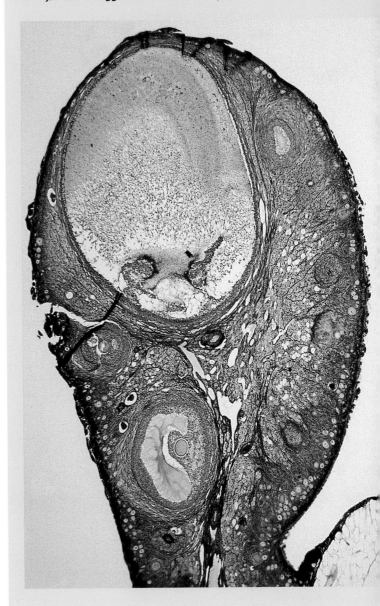

MALE REPRODUCTIVE ORGANS

Male system

The main parts of the male reproductive system, also called the sex organs, are the testes, epididymes, sperm ducts (vas deferens or ductus deferens), seminal glands (seminal vesicles), prostate gland and penis. Unlike the female reproductive parts, which are within the lower abdomen, some of the male parts are below the abdomen, with the testes contained in a bag-like pouch of skin called the scrotum.

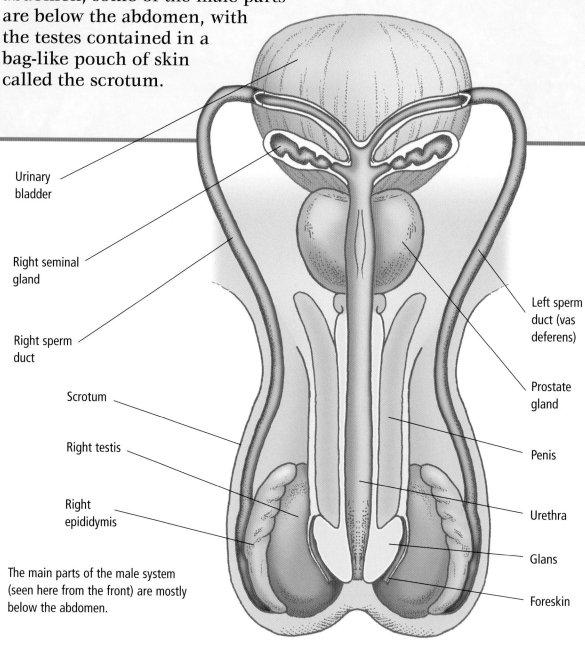

Urinary bladder

Right seminal gland

Right sperm duct

Scrotum

Right testis

Right epididymis

Left sperm duct (vas deferens)

Prostate gland

Penis

Urethra

Glans

Foreskin

The main parts of the male system (seen here from the front) are mostly below the abdomen.

The male dolphin's sexual parts are under a pocket-like flap of skin, to make the body more streamlined.

ANIMAL VERSUS HUMAN

In the human, the sperm-making testes are outside the main lower body or abdomen. In many animals the testes are contained within the abdomen. In a male dolphin the penis is also partly contained within the abdomen, covered by a flap of skin. This creates a smooth, streamlined body shape when swimming.

THE TESTES

Each of the two rounded testes (testicles) is four to five centimetres across. Inside, millions of sperm are produced every day (see page 14). They pass into the epididymis, which is a very thin tube about six metres long, joined to the upper and outer side of the testis and coiled tightly around it. From each epididymis another thin tube, the sperm duct, carries sperm towards the penis.

TUBES AND GLANDS

Each sperm duct goes from its epididymis up into the lower abdomen, where it meets and joins a tube from the thumb-sized seminal gland. This happens on each side of the body. The left and right tubes join and lead through the middle of the prostate gland where yet another tube joins them – the urethra. This comes from the bladder just above the prostate gland. The seminal and prostate glands add nourishment-containing fluid to the sperm cells, before they leave the body along the urethra. This runs along the middle of the penis and opens at its end or tip. At different times the urethra carries different substances – sperm cells in their semen or seminal fluid during sex (see page 16), or urine from the bladder during urination.

Millions of cells

The male reproductive system produces millions of sperm cells every day. The process begins in the testis or testicle, which is made of many small, tightly coiled tubes called seminiferous tubules. There are 600–800 in each testis and their lengths added together would be more than 200 metres.

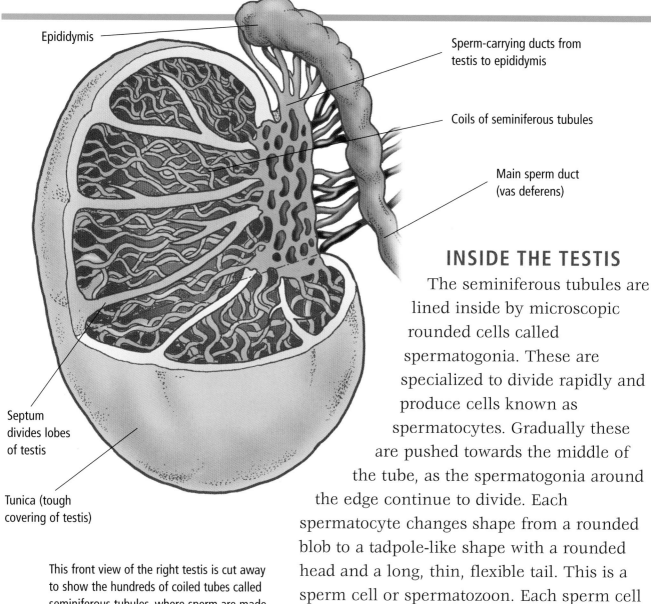

Epididymis

Sperm-carrying ducts from testis to epididymis

Coils of seminiferous tubules

Main sperm duct (vas deferens)

Septum divides lobes of testis

Tunica (tough covering of testis)

This front view of the right testis is cut away to show the hundreds of coiled tubes called seminiferous tubules, where sperm are made and become mature.

INSIDE THE TESTIS

The seminiferous tubules are lined inside by microscopic rounded cells called spermatogonia. These are specialized to divide rapidly and produce cells known as spermatocytes. Gradually these are pushed towards the middle of the tube, as the spermatogonia around the edge continue to divide. Each spermatocyte changes shape from a rounded blob to a tadpole-like shape with a rounded head and a long, thin, flexible tail. This is a sperm cell or spermatozoon. Each sperm cell takes about two months to develop.

MICRO-BODY

Each of the seminiferous tubules in the testis is about 50 centimetres long but only one-fifth of a millimetre wide. Inside, spermatogonia cells around the edge multiply to make spermatocytes, which gradually change shape to form tadpole-like sperm cells near the centre.

This microphotograph shows sperm cells in stages of development (blue), those in the centre with long tails, within the narrow seminiferous tubule (pale orange).

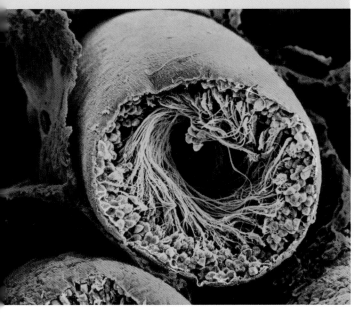

EPIDIDYMIS

As sperm cells form they pass along the fluid in the middle of the seminiferous tubules, which join to the single tube of the epididymis, coiled around the testis. Here the sperm cells become fully ripe and are stored for up to a month. If they do not leave the body through the penis they slowly break down into tiny pieces. The whole process of sperm production is controlled by the hormone testosterone, made in the testes. In turn, the production of testosterone is controlled by two hormones, follicle stimulating hormone and luteinizing hormone, made by the tiny pituitary gland at the base of the brain (see page 8).

weblinks▸

To find out more about sperm production, go to:
www.waylinks.co.uk/series/ourbodies/reproduction

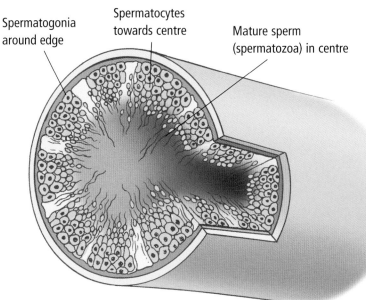

Spermatogonia around edge

Spermatocytes towards centre

Mature sperm (spermatozoa) in centre

A close-up of a seminiferous tubule shows how rounded spermatogonia develop into mature sperm cells (right).

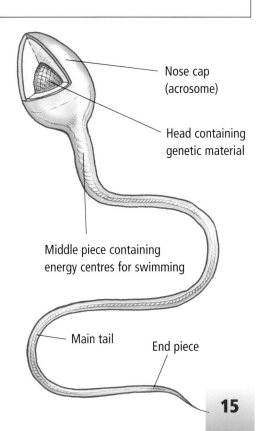

Nose cap (acrosome)

Head containing genetic material

Middle piece containing energy centres for swimming

Main tail

End piece

THE REPRODUCTIVE PROCESS

Crucial timing

A new human begins when a ripe egg cell joins a mature sperm cell, to form a fertilized egg. There are various events which must take place so that this can happen, and their timing is very important.

MICRO-BODY

The egg cell is smaller than the dot on this i, but it is still many times larger than the sperm cells. Many sperm swarm around the egg, but when one sperm has joined with it, a barrier hardens around the egg to prevent other sperm reaching it.

Dozens of sperm cells (cream colour) swarm around the huge egg cell (blue) and try to join or fuse head-first with it. Only one will succeed.

JOURNEY OF THE SPERM

Sperm leave the male body by a process called ejaculation. This involves the tightening or contraction of muscles around the epididymis, prostate gland, and seminiferous tubules, which pushes sperm cells from the two testes and epididymes, along the sperm ducts into the urethra.

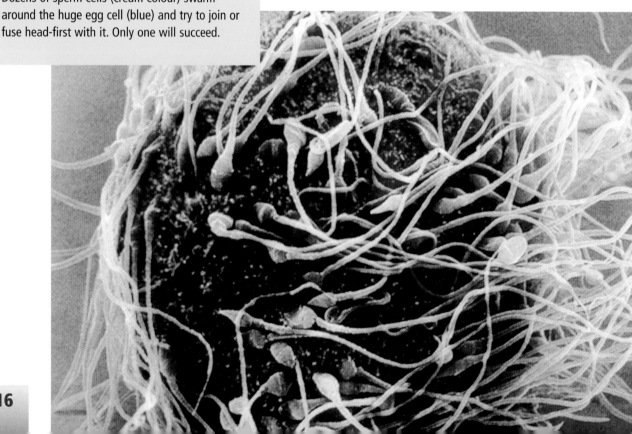

There are about 300–500 million sperm cells, in nourishment-packed fluids from the seminal and prostate glands. The tadpole-shaped sperm lash their long, thin tails and swim on their journey, out of the tip of the penis. During sexual intercourse when the penis is in the vagina of the female body, the sperm are released into its upper part. From here the sperm swim through the cervix into the uterus. Throughout the journey, millions of sperm cells die.

JOURNEY OF THE EGG

Usually, an egg cell is ripe and able to join with a sperm cell for only one to two days after ovulation. Unlike sperm cells, the egg cell cannot actively swim. It moves very slowly along the oviduct, wafted along by tiny hairs called cilia in the lining of the tube. Meanwhile the sperm swim from the uterus into the two oviducts. Of the millions that began the journey, perhaps several thousands reach the ripe egg cell in one of the oviducts. Just one of these sperm cells joins with the egg, at fertilization.

TWINS

If one egg is fertilized and then divides, and each of these two cells develops into a baby, the result is two babies with the same genetic material – identical twins. If two eggs are

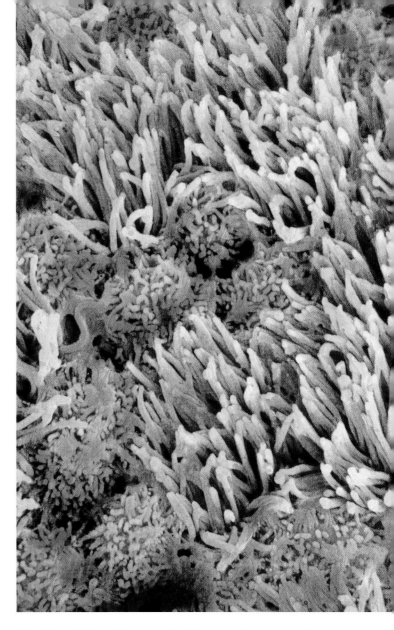

The lining of the oviduct (egg duct), between the ovary and uterus, has millions of waving micro-hairs called cilia (yellow). Scattered between them are secretory cells (purple) which make fluids and mucus to smooth the egg's passage.

released together, and each is fertilized by a sperm, the result is non-identical twins. These children are as similar to each other as any sisters or brothers born to the same parents.

weblinks

To find out more about the reproductive process, go to: www.waylinks.co.uk/series/ourbodies/reproduction

THE FIRST WEEK

Instructions for development

The egg cell and sperm cell each contain tiny threads known as chromosomes, which carry chemicals of the substance DNA, arranged into groups called genes. These contain the instructions for how the baby will grow and develop – for instance, whether it will be male or female, and have light or dark skin, or brown or blue eyes. Most cells in the human body have 23 pairs of chromosomes. The egg and sperm each have only 23 – one of each pair. When an egg and sperm join together, they complete the 23 pairs of chromosomes to make the full set of genes for the new baby.

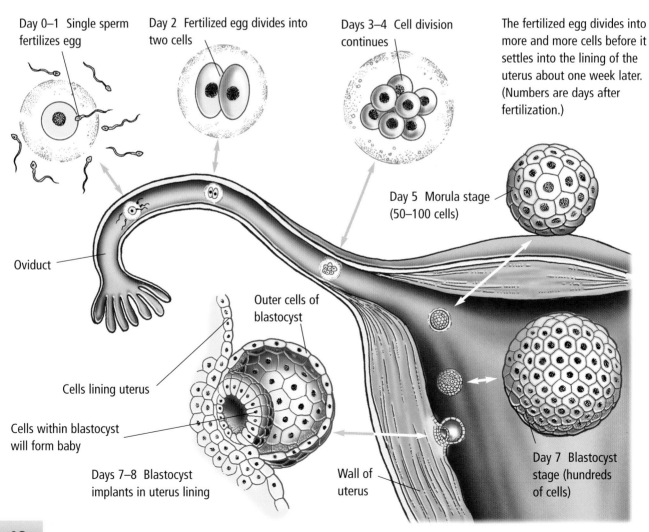

Day 0–1 Single sperm fertilizes egg

Day 2 Fertilized egg divides into two cells

Days 3–4 Cell division continues

The fertilized egg divides into more and more cells before it settles into the lining of the uterus about one week later. (Numbers are days after fertilization.)

Day 5 Morula stage (50–100 cells)

Oviduct

Outer cells of blastocyst

Cells lining uterus

Cells within blastocyst will form baby

Days 7–8 Blastocyst implants in uterus lining

Wall of uterus

Day 7 Blastocyst stage (hundreds of cells)

FROM OVIDUCT TO UTERUS

After one or two days, the fertilized egg cell divides in half, into two cells. About 12 hours later these two cells also divide, forming four cells. Then the same happens, to give eight cells, 16 and so on. This gradually forms a tiny, blackberry-like ball of cells, still passing slowly along the oviduct. After about 5–7 days there are 100-plus cells in the ball shape with a hollow, fluid-filled centre. This is the blastocyst. The original egg cell was so much bigger than other types of cell that only now, after many divisions, the cells of the blastocyst reach normal body cell size.

IMPLANTATION

Seven or eight days after fertilization the blastocyst settles into the thickened lining of the uterus, where it receives nourishment for further growth and development. This stage is known as implantation. The cells continue to divide, and now also start to grow, using nutrients from the uterus lining around them. The blastocyst begins to develop rapidly into a tiny baby. The whole process of fertilization, implantation and the start of pregnancy is called conception.

The main pale, shadowy object in the centre of this micro-photograph is a six-day blastocyst, with the individual cells just visible as fuzzy outlines. (The other cells to the top left are from the original egg's outer covering.)

Top Tips

The healthy development of the tiny baby depends greatly on the mother's health. Harmful chemicals such as drugs, tobacco smoke or alcohol can interfere with the baby's development during pregnancy. So pregnant women should not take drugs (even medicines, unless advised to by a doctor), drink alcohol, smoke, or spend time in smoky rooms. A woman who may become pregnant should also take care to eat a healthy diet and perhaps take supplements such as folic acid, as advised by a doctor, to help ensure the baby is healthy.

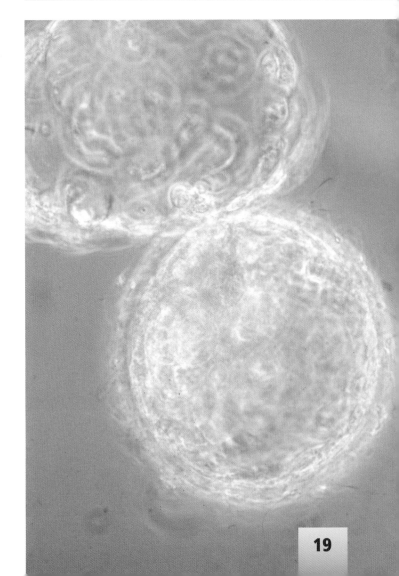

REPRODUCTIVE PROBLEMS

A number of reasons

There are many reasons why sex does not always lead to pregnancy, when the couple wish for pregnancy to happen. They include problems with when sex takes place, or with the man's or woman's reproductive system.

Surgeon's eyepiece

TIMING

The egg cell is alive and healthy, and able to join with a sperm, only for a day or two after ovulation. So for conception to happen, sperm cells must be present in the female reproductive parts at this time. Also, the sperm themselves can survive in the female reproductive parts for only three to four days. So usually, sex must happen a day or two either before or after ovulation, for the egg to be fertilized (see pages 16–17).

Intestines and other abdominal organs

Ovary and oviduct within abdomen

A laparoscope is a device used to see inside the abdomen, carry out treatment and perhaps collect eggs for IVF (see opposite).

IN THE MALE

Only one sperm is needed to fertilize the egg, but millions are required to ensure that this happens. If the man produces fewer than 20–30 million sperm each time, the chances of conception can be greatly reduced. This 'low sperm count' has many causes, from a previous illness or injury to stress or tiredness, or taking various drugs, including alcohol and some medical drugs. Advice from a doctor, and perhaps medicines to increase sperm production, can usually help.

IN THE FEMALE

In some women, hormonal control of the female cycle does not work properly, so that an egg does not ripen, or is not ovulated, or the lining of the womb is not prepared. Or previous illness or infection in the lower abdomen, known as the pelvic region, can damage the ovaries, oviducts or other reproductive parts. A general term for this is PID, pelvic inflammatory disease. There are many treatments for such problems, ranging from medical drugs and hormones to various operations. Another option is to collect eggs and sperm so that they join outside the body, then place fertilized eggs into the woman's uterus. This is IVF, in vitro fertilization.

Top Tips

The male's main reproductive parts are outside the abdomen and easily damaged. During risky activities, including many sports, boys and men are advised to wear protective equipment such as an athletic support or jockstrap. An injury may affect sperm production and the ability to become a father.

A medical worker watches a microscope image on a monitor screen, of an egg cell being held on the end of a glass tube called a pipette (visible on the left of the screen). The needle (to the right) will inject the genetic material from a sperm directly into the egg.

THE EARLY EMBRYO

Dividing cells

About ten days after fertilization, the tiny ball of cells known as the embryo has settled into the thickened lining of the uterus. Its cells continue to divide and grow and start to form a small disc inside the ball. This will become the baby itself, while the layers around it will become the bag-like containers or membranes within the uterus (see page 26).

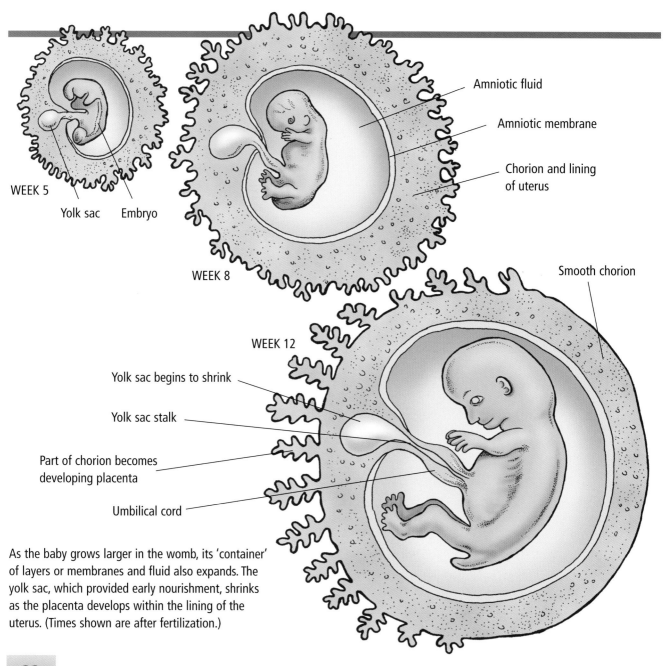

WEEK 5

Yolk sac   Embryo

WEEK 8

Amniotic fluid

Amniotic membrane

Chorion and lining of uterus

Smooth chorion

WEEK 12

Yolk sac begins to shrink

Yolk sac stalk

Part of chorion becomes developing placenta

Umbilical cord

As the baby grows larger in the womb, its 'container' of layers or membranes and fluid also expands. The yolk sac, which provided early nourishment, shrinks as the placenta develops within the lining of the uterus. (Times shown are after fertilization.)

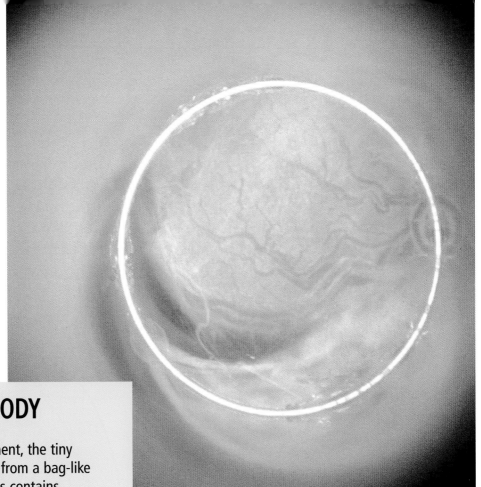

This view into the womb shows the yolk sac at about four weeks after fertilization. Blood vessels over its surface carry its nourishment to the tiny baby (which is not in this view).

MICRO-BODY

During very early development, the tiny embryo gains nourishment from a bag-like part called the yolk sac. This contains nutrient-rich yellow yolk, similar to the yolk in a hen's egg. From six weeks after fertilization, the yolk sac shrinks away, and the embryo is nourished through the placenta (see pages 26–27).

THE BODY TAKES SHAPE

Two weeks after fertilization the tiny disc of the embryo is less than one millimetre across. Its cells continue to divide and grow, into hundreds and then thousands. They also begin to move about and build the shape of the new baby. About three weeks after fertilization the embryo is the size and shape of this c. Yet inside its tiny body, parts such as the heart and brain are forming. After four weeks, the head is taking shape, and tiny bumps called limb buds appear on the body, which will grow into arms and legs. The whole embryo would fit into this O.

THE SECOND MONTH

During the second month, development of the baby continues very rapidly. The head is large compared to the body as the brain, eyes, ears and mouth form. Major body parts such as the lungs, stomach, intestines and muscles are also taking shape. About eight weeks after fertilization, the whole embryo is hardly larger than a grape. Yet all its major body parts have formed, even its eyelids, fingers and toes.

The changing fetus

After two months in the uterus, the developing baby is no longer known as an embryo, but as a fetus. It has all its major body parts and organs, and its heart has begun to beat. During the next seven months the main changes will be an increase in size, and the formation of smaller body features like eyelashes, fingernails and toenails.

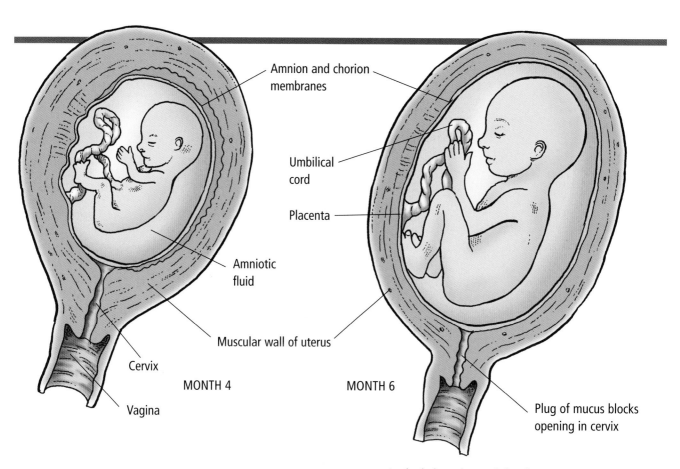

Amnion and chorion membranes

Umbilical cord

Placenta

Amniotic fluid

Muscular wall of uterus

Cervix

MONTH 4

Vagina

MONTH 6

Plug of mucus blocks opening in cervix

As the baby enlarges, it has less room to move inside the uterus. (Times shown are after fertilization.) The mother usually notices her abdomen beginning to bulge from the fourth month.

THE MIDDLE THIRD

During the middle third of pregnancy, months four to six, the fetus continues to grow rapidly, from 30 millimetres in length to almost 300. During the fourth month, its reproductive parts become visible on the outside of its body, so it is possible to see, using a scan or similar method of imaging, if the baby is a girl or boy. Blood is flowing through the blood vessels, and a covering of thin, fine hair begins to grow on the body.

MONTHS FIVE AND SIX

During the fifth month the muscles and skeleton become stronger. The fetus begins to move – simple stretching at first, then more controlled movements such as kicking the legs and clenching the fingers. The heart pumps blood at the rate of about 150 beats per minute. During the sixth month the fetus grows rapidly longer and looks slim or lean. Its movements become more complicated, and even include thumb-sucking. The skin is covered by a slippery, creamy layer of a substance called vernix. Small body details continue to form, such as the eyebrows.

By the ninth and last month in the uterus, the baby is very cramped. It has usually turned upside down, ready to be born head-first.

ANIMAL VERSUS HUMAN

Compared to a new human baby, a new baby marsupial like a possum is tiny and at an early stage of development. Born after only about 17 days inside its mother, it is smaller than a grape, with no fur, closed eyes and ears, and paddle-like legs. It crawls to the mother's pouch, where it spends five more months continuing its development.

This newborn brush-tailed possum is drinking milk from its mother's teat, inside her pouch.

LIFE SUPPORT IN THE WOMB

Protective layers

Inside the uterus (womb), it is dark and quiet. The developing baby is surrounded by a liquid called amniotic fluid, and two thin, bag-like layers of membranes, the amnion and chorion. In the early stages when the fetus is very small, it can float about in its fluid and membranes. But after about six to seven months, the baby becomes cramped and cannot stretch easily. Although the uterus continues to enlarge around it, the baby has much less room for movement.

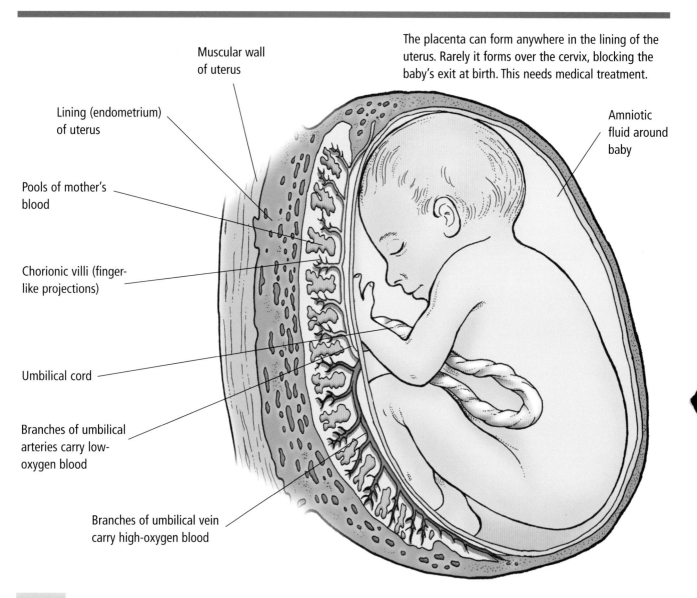

Muscular wall of uterus

The placenta can form anywhere in the lining of the uterus. Rarely it forms over the cervix, blocking the baby's exit at birth. This needs medical treatment.

Lining (endometrium) of uterus

Amniotic fluid around baby

Pools of mother's blood

Chorionic villi (finger-like projections)

Umbilical cord

Branches of umbilical arteries carry low-oxygen blood

Branches of umbilical vein carry high-oxygen blood

VITAL NEEDS

In the uterus, the baby cannot feed itself, or breathe air. Nutrients and oxygen come from the mother's body, through a part called the placenta (afterbirth). This is shaped like a plate and it develops in part of the thickened lining of the uterus. The baby's blood flows to the placenta along two vessels (tubes), the umbilical arteries, within a rope-like part, the umbilical cord. Blood in these arteries takes oxygen and nutrients from the mother's blood in the placenta and passes waste substances from the baby in the opposite direction. The baby's blood then flows along another vessel in the cord, the umbilical vein, back to the baby's body.

CHANGES IN THE MOTHER

The first sign that a woman is pregnant is usually when her next period (menstrual bleeding) does not occur. Hormonal changes keep the lining of the womb thickened, to nourish the tiny embryo. By the fourth month of pregnancy the mother can feel and see her enlarged uterus, and by five months, she can detect the baby moving. She also gains weight due to the baby itself and also the fluids, membranes, placenta, enlarged uterus and other parts.

Towards the end of pregnancy, the baby and uterus push the mother's abdominal organs up against her chest, and the extra weight at the front affects her posture.

weblinks

To find out more about life support in the womb, go to:
www.waylinks.co.uk/series/ourbodies/reproduction

MICRO-BODY

Inside the placenta, the baby's blood flows through tiny tubes surrounded by the mother's blood. The two sets of blood do not mix, but nutrients and oxygen can easily pass through the thin layer separating them.

Growing in size

During the last couple of months of pregnancy, the mother's abdomen enlarges greatly as the baby and uterus get bigger. They press upwards on her chest, so she may become short of breath, particularly when lying down or when walking or exercising. The mother's breasts enlarge as they prepare to produce milk to feed the newborn baby. By the eighth month of pregnancy, the typical baby is about 450 millimetres long and weighs 2.5 kilograms. However the mother's enlarged uterus with its fluids and membranes, along with other bodily changes, mean she has gained about nine kilograms.

In most regions the ultrasound scan is a routine check during pregnancy.

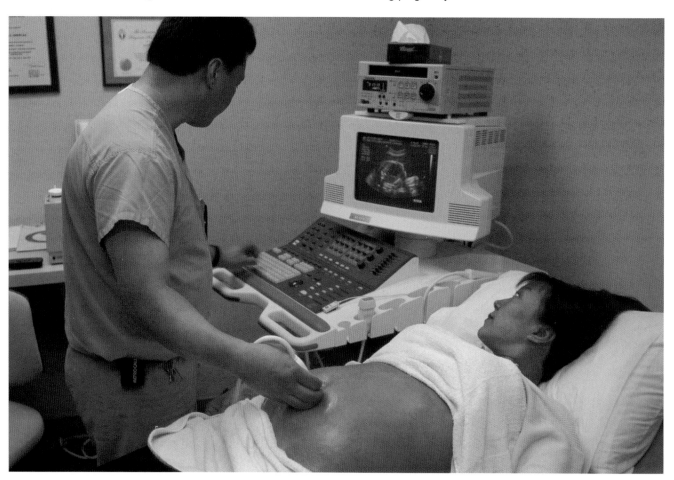

MICRO-BODY

During pregnancy the mother's breasts enlarge as the mammary glands grow bigger within them. The glands are packed with large cells that make and release milk. The milk then passes along tubes called lactiferous ducts to the nipple, the darker, raised part of the breast. When the newborn baby sucks the nipple, milk will be released.

Milk-making cells are arranged in curved layers (dark pink/purple), each enclosing a central space (very pale pink). Many of the central spaces here contain blobs of milk and other products (mid pink).

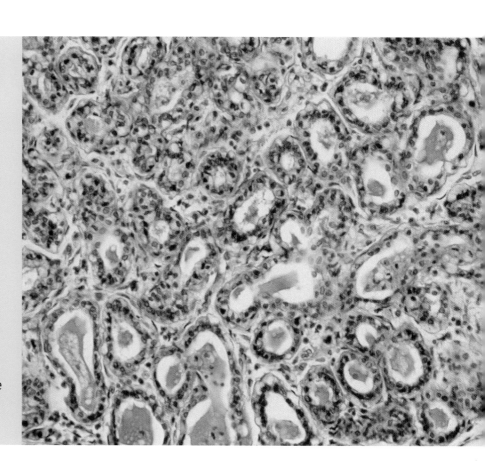

SEEING THE UNBORN BABY

In many regions, pregnant women attend a health centre or medical clinic for regular prenatal ('before-birth') checks. Usually a type of body scan called an ultrasound is carried out to ensure the baby is developing normally. The timing of this varies from place to place; in the UK it is advised at around 20 weeks. The scanner beams ultrasound waves (too high-pitched for us to hear) into the mother's abdomen. These bounce off the baby and other parts inside, and a computer analyzes the reflections or echoes to form a picture of the baby in the uterus. The mother may also be offered blood tests to ensure the baby is healthy.

THE LAST MONTH

By the last month of pregnancy, the hair on the baby's head has usually started to grow, and the baby looks increasingly 'chubby' because of a thickening layer of fat under its skin. Around this time the baby usually turns upside down, ready to emerge from the uterus head-first. This is a safe way to be born since the rounded head gradually stretches open the cervix and birth canal, and then the body, arms and legs follow without getting stuck or crossed over.

THE DAY OF BIRTH

THE ROLE OF HORMONES

Pregnancy is closely controlled by hormones in the mother's body. The main hormone is hCG, human chorionic gonadotrophin. It is made in the placenta and keeps the uterus and placenta developing properly. The typical 'pregnancy test' sometimes used to confirm conception comprises chemicals that detect hCG in the mother's blood or urine.

LABOUR

As the day of birth approaches at about nine months, another hormone takes over. This is oxytocin, released into the mother's blood by the pituitary gland at the base of her brain. Oxytocin causes the powerful muscles in the stretched walls of the uterus to shorten or contract. This presses the baby against the cervix (uterine opening). At first the contractions occur every 20–30 minutes. Gradually they become more powerful and frequent, coming every 3–5 minutes. This time is called the first stage of labour, or simply 'labour'. The bag-like membranes around the baby tear and allow the fluid in the uterus to flow out of the vagina, known as 'breaking of the waters'.

BIRTH

The baby's head presses harder on the cervix, which opens wider. Eventually the baby's head can begin to pass through, out of the uterus and into the birth canal. Strong contractions continue and push the baby along the birth canal, to emerge into

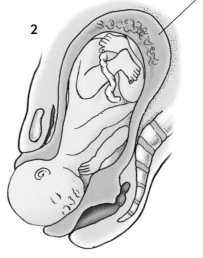

1

As labour progresses, the baby's head presses on the cervix, which is becoming wider or dilated.

Cervix

Uterine muscles contract

2

Eventually the cervix is wide enough for the baby's head to pass through, into the birth canal.

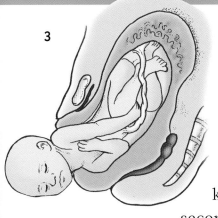

3

The baby's shoulders follow as delivery proceeds and the baby is born.

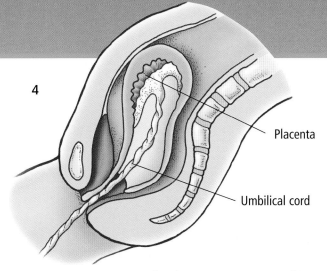

4

Placenta

Umbilical cord

the outside world. This is known as the second stage of labour, or delivery. Soon after, the placenta comes away from the inner lining of the uterus and also emerges. This is the third stage or afterbirth. When the baby is safely born, the umbilical cord linking it to the placenta is clamped or cut.

The placenta comes away and is also expelled from the uterus.

weblinks

To find out more about birth, go to:
www.waylinks.co.uk/series/ourbodies/reproduction

After a strenuous and tiring birth, the new baby meets its mother face to face.

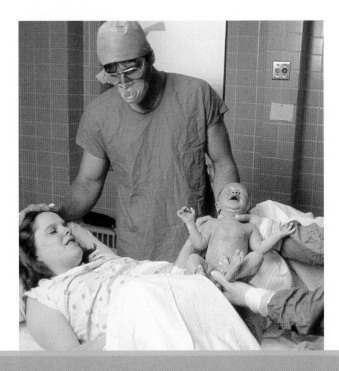

ANIMAL VERSUS HUMAN

The time taken for a human birth varies hugely. On average, it is 14–15 hours for a mother's first baby, and less for further pregnancies. In many animals, it happens much faster. An antelope or gazelle gives birth in 15–30 minutes, and after another 30 minutes, the youngster is able to run. This speedy birth means the mother and baby antelope are at risk from predators such as lions for the shortest possible time.

Baby deer, like this white-tailed deer fawn, must be able to run from danger as soon as possible.

A NEW BABY

The first breath

Birth is extremely tiring for both mother and baby. As the baby emerges it sees lights, hears loud noises and feels fresh air, all for the first time. The sudden changes may cause it to cry loudly. Crying opens the baby's air passages and lungs, helping the baby to breathe for itself. This is helpful, given that the baby's supply of oxygen from the placenta will soon cease, because the placenta has broken away from the uterus and the umbilical cord has been clamped or cut.

It usually takes a few attempts for both the mother and the baby to get used to breastfeeding. But soon it becomes a natural routine, and valuable time spent together.

FEEDING

After birth, the baby no longer receives nourishment through the placenta, so it must use its digestive system. The most natural way for the baby to feed is to suck milk from the mother's mammary glands in her breasts. The production of milk is controlled by a hormone called prolactin, while the release of milk from the breasts as the baby sucks is controlled by oxytocin. Both these hormones come from the mother's pituitary gland.

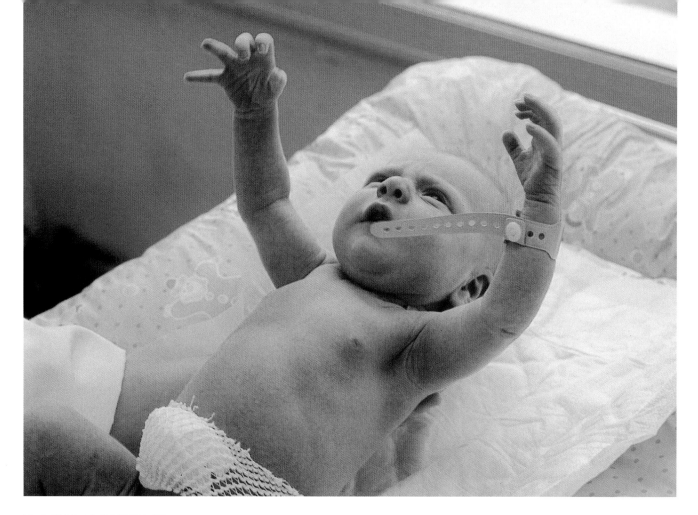

DAILY ROUTINE

The new baby sleeps for 18–20 hours out of every 24. It usually wakes up and perhaps cries, only when hungry, hot, cold or uncomfortable, for example, in need of cleaning and nappy changing. The new baby cannot control its bladder or bowels, and so empties these when they are full, by an automatic body reaction called a reflex. The baby has other reflexes too. If startled by a sudden movement or loud noise, it throws its arms out and cries. It will also grip an object placed in its hand. These reflexes and other body processes are tested as part of the postnatal ('after birth') check-up by medical staff, to ensure the baby is healthy.

If a new baby is lowered briefly and quickly, as part of its check-up, it shows a startle reflex by throwing out its arms and legs, trying to grab with its hands, and crying out. This reflex continues until about two to three months of age.

Try this!

If you know a new baby, ask the baby's parents if you can touch its cheek very gently with your finger. The baby turns its head towards your finger, its lips ready to suck. This automatic reaction is the rooting or sucking reflex, and it helps the baby to find the mother's nipple and feed on milk.

BIRTH PROBLEMS

Physical changes

Birth is a stressful and complicated time, with many changes in both the baby and mother. It is also a very physical event. The pregnant mother's uterus is the largest and most powerful muscle in her body, and as it contracts strongly, the baby is squeezed with considerable force through the birth canal. The skull bones inside the baby's head are not yet joined together or fully hardened. As the baby leaves the uterus, the bones can bend and move slightly while still protecting the brain inside. This allows the head, which is the baby's widest part, to change shape so it can slide more easily through the cervix and birth canal.

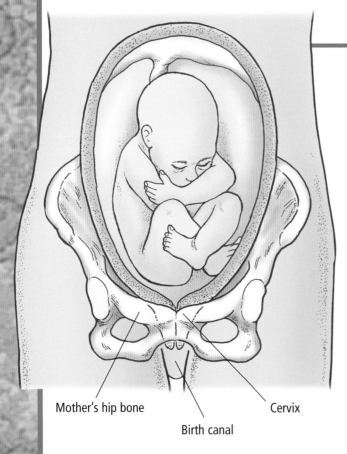

Mother's hip bone

Cervix

Birth canal

In a breech (bottom-first) presentation the baby may be facing the front, as shown here, or side-on, or facing its mother's back.

PROBLEM PRESENTATIONS

Most babies are born head first (see page 31), and this is known as cephalic presentation. However in some cases the baby's shoulder tries to emerge first, or even its bottom, which is called breech presentation. Coming out of the uterus in these positions is much more awkward and the baby may get stuck. Doctors may be able to twist the baby into the correct position, or use spoon-like devices called forceps to ease it out. In some cases an operation may be necessary. In a caesarean section, doctors make careful incisions or cuts through the walls of the mother's abdomen and uterus, remove the baby and then sew up the incisions. This operation may also be used to remove a baby which has become ill before birth.

PREMATURE BABIES

A baby born before the usual time of nine months is said to be premature. The earlier it is born, the smaller and weaker it usually is, and in need of special care. It may be kept warm in a box-like container called an incubator, and provided with extra oxygen to help its breathing. However babies born less than one month premature are not usually in great danger.

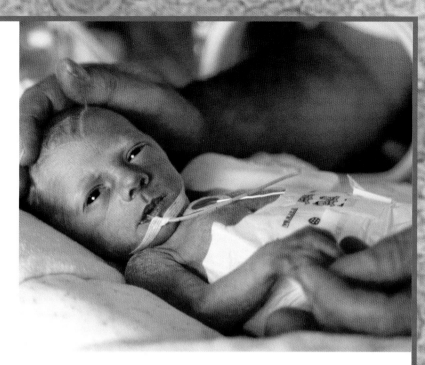

A premature baby may be fitted with sensors to monitor its heartbeat, and perhaps a mouth tube for fluids.

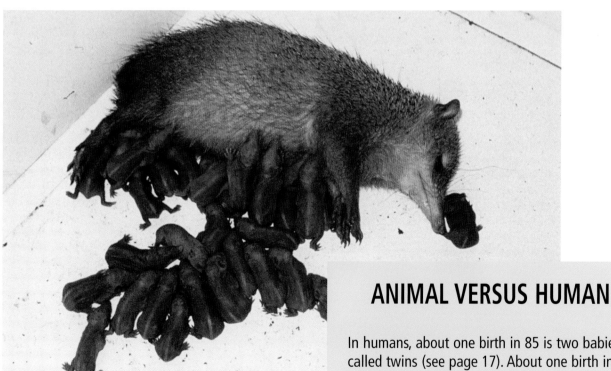

The tenrec is a shrew-like animal from Madagascar. It may have more than 20 babies in one litter, but many soon die.

ANIMAL VERSUS HUMAN

In humans, about one birth in 85 is two babies, called twins (see page 17). About one birth in 7,500 is three babies, or triplets, and one in half a million is four babies, or quadruplets. Some animal mothers usually have many more babies at one time – in rare cases, more than 30!

GROWING UP

Infancy

The period of infancy lasts from about one month after birth until the young child can walk, which is, on average, at one year of age. The body grows faster during infancy than at any other time after birth. Most healthy babies weigh three times more at one year old than they did at birth. In particular the baby's brain almost doubles in weight, from about one-quarter to one-half of its eventual adult size.

MOTOR SKILLS

Learning new knowledge, skills and abilities does not begin at school. It happens from birth, and is incredibly rapid during infancy. Part of this learning involves movements and actions. After three months a typical baby can reach out and grasp a toy or other object, and roll over when lying down. By six months it sits up unaided and puts food, or anything else it is holding, into its mouth. By nine months it may crawl on hands and knees, and begin to stand up while holding a support. These physical abilities are known as motor skills. They depend on fast development of many body parts, including muscles, nerves, and especially the brain, which controls and coordinates the movements.

Eating may seem easy now, but at the age of one or two, it's a very tricky process – and messy to learn!

MENTAL ABILITIES

An infant also develops many new mental or mind-based skills. As early as six weeks of age, it learns that if it smiles at a human face, it will get a response as people smile and talk back. The infant improves its abilities to look and listen, and learns to recognize familiar faces and voices. By a year old, a typical infant can say a few simple words such as names of family members or pets.

— **weblinks** —

To find out more about growing up, go to:
www.waylinks.co.uk/series/ourbodies/reproduction

Babies rapidly learn to identify their close family members by sights, sounds and smells too. They also learn that if they smile, they will get a reaction and more attention.

Try this!

An infant's change of diet, from milk to other foods or 'solids', is called weaning. It happens at widely differing ages, often not just for the nutritional needs of the baby itself, but for reasons of the parents' tradition, culture or lifestyle. In general, young children prefer fairly sweet foods. Ask family members and friends of different ages which foods they like, such as ice cream, chocolate, onions or spicy dishes like chilli. Is there a gradual change with age, from preferring sweet foods to stronger-flavoured spicy or savoury ones?

THE YOUNG CHILD

Slowing down and speeding up

Between the ages of one and five years, the body's rate of growth gradually slows. But learning physical and mental skills gets ever faster. Inside the brain, thousands of new connections form every day between its various parts. These represent memories such as words and names, the appearances of people and places, and the ability to carry out actions and movements. By 15–18 months a typical young child can use a spoon at mealtimes, kick and throw a ball, and control the bladder reflex while awake, so that urination happens only at certain times. By four years old the child is able to get dressed and undressed, hop and skip, and talk in full sentences.

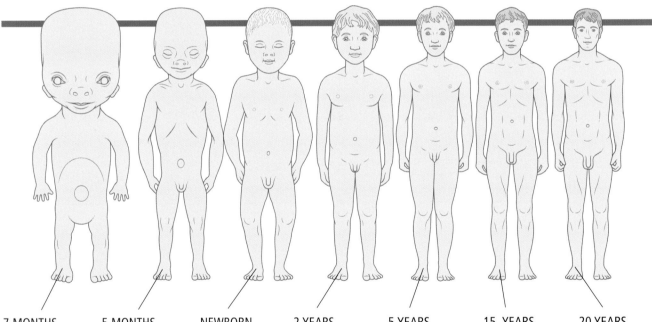

7 MONTHS BEFORE BIRTH
The brain grows very early in development, making the head of the fetus look huge.

5 MONTHS BEFORE BIRTH
The fetus's head is still very large, and the arms are growing faster than the legs.

NEWBORN
The head is twice as big, compared to the rest of the body, as it will be in the adult.

2 YEARS
Arms, legs and main body are all about equal length, making the head look smaller.

5 YEARS
The legs are starting to grow faster now and soon become longer than the arms.

15 YEARS
The head forms about one-sixth of the total body height as the legs grow fastest.

20 YEARS
Full size is attained, and in most adults, legs make up almost half the total height.

In these diagrams of growth at different stages, before and after birth, all the bodies are drawn to the same overall height. This shows how the proportions change – especially the size of the head relative to the body and legs.

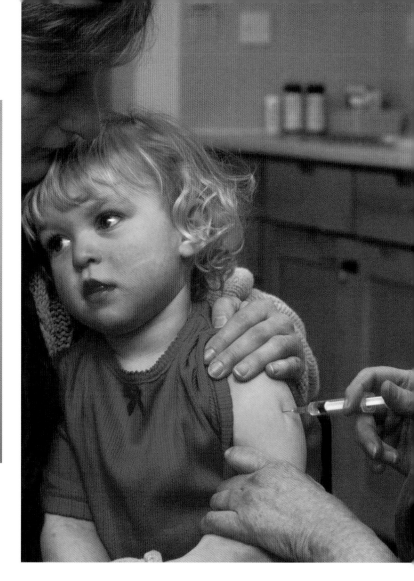

Immunization may bring a moment's tearfulness, but for most children (except in special circumstances) it also gives years of protection against infectious diseases, which can be disabling or even deadly.

PROTECTION AGAINST DISEASE

Many kinds of harmful microbes or germs can invade the body and cause illness. For some of these, once the body has suffered the illness and recovered, the next time it encounters the germs, it can kill them very quickly before they cause disease. This ability to recognize and fight disease is called resistance or immunity. In vaccination or immunization, harmless versions of the germs (or the chemicals they produce) are put into the body, usually by injection. The body does not suffer from the illness, but it does develop immunity against it.

CHILDHOOD IMMUNIZATIONS

Most babies and children receive a carefully planned series of immunizations to protect them against possibly dangerous diseases in future. The times of the injections and the diseases vary, but they may include polio, diphtheria, tetanus, pertussis (whooping cough), measles, mumps, rubella (German measles) and perhaps tuberculosis (TB).

THE OLDER CHILD

Developing skills

Throughout childhood, to the age of about 10–12 years, the body's growth rate gradually slows down. However its mental or mind-based progress increases at great speed. A young child learns in many different ways. He or she develops language skills such as understanding new words, and putting them together in a meaningful way as sentences. Further physical abilities and motor skills rely on the increasing coordination of body muscles, such as learning how to draw, write, ride a bicycle or play a musical instrument.

Team sports encourage children to stay healthy, and also to work with others and cooperate as part of a group, to achieve their goal.

BEHAVIOURAL CHANGES

There are also huge developments in behaviour – what the child thinks, says and does, and how she or he gets on with family and friends. Younger children tend to think mainly of themselves, want whatever they see at once, and ignore the wishes of others. Gradually they learn how to share, interact with others and make friends. This type of learning does not take place only in nurseries and schools. It is 'learning from life, for life' and takes place at home, when playing, out shopping, in the car, taking part in sports – indeed, just about anywhere. All of these advances contribute to the growth and development of the child's whole body.

HEALTH CHECKS

Development during childhood can be measured at arranged check-ups with health workers and medical staff. But a child's growth can also be monitored in a less formal, official way by parents and family members. If there is cause for concern, for example, if a child is slow in learning to talk or read, expert advice should be obtained sooner rather than later. Usually there is no great problem and the child soon catches up as part of the normal variation between people. But if there is a significant problem, then early help is likely to be more successful.

---

weblinks

To find out more about childhood growth, go to:
www.waylinks.co.uk/series/ourbodies/reproduction

MICRO-BODY

Apart from the brain, the body parts which change most during childhood are the bones of the skeleton. In a young child the 'bones' are partly made of cartilage (gristle), which is slightly softer and bendier. It is less likely to break during knocks and falls – which children suffer often. Gradually the cartilage parts of the bones harden into true bone, by 18–20 years of age.

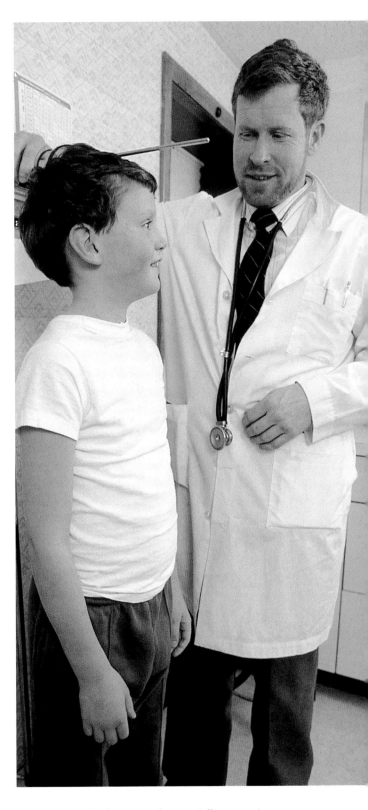

A regular check on growth, especially measuring height and weight, takes just a few minutes. It gives reassurance that all is well – or detects any problem early, so it can be dealt with sooner.

Puberty

When a baby is born, the only parts of its body which are not working are the reproductive parts. These begin to develop fully after childhood, and the body's growth also speeds up greatly at this time, which is called puberty. The age of puberty varies greatly – it may start anywhere between nine and 16 years old. The process usually occurs a year or two earlier in girls than boys, and takes a shorter time in girls, two to three years, compared with three to four in a boy.

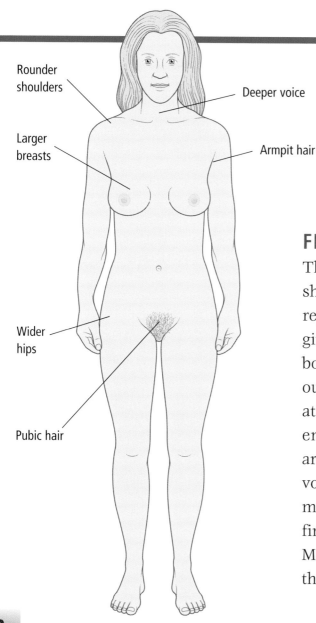

Rounder shoulders

Deeper voice

Larger breasts

Armpit hair

Wider hips

Pubic hair

Most girls go through the same physical changes during puberty, in the same sequence. However there is huge variation in the times at which these occur, and some changes are less marked in certain women compared to others.

FEMALE CHANGES

Through childhood, the overall size and shape of the body (apart from the reproductive parts) is much the same in girls and boys. During puberty, the female body grows rapidly in height, then its outline becomes more rounded, especially at the shoulders and hips. The breasts enlarge, hair grows under the arms and around the vulva and vagina, and the voice deepens slightly. The female or menstrual cycle gradually begins, with the first full cycle known as the menarche. Most of these changes are controlled by the hormone oestrogen from the ovaries.

Adolescence is the phase of life which includes puberty, and for most people, corresponds to the teenage years. It is a time of increasing independence.

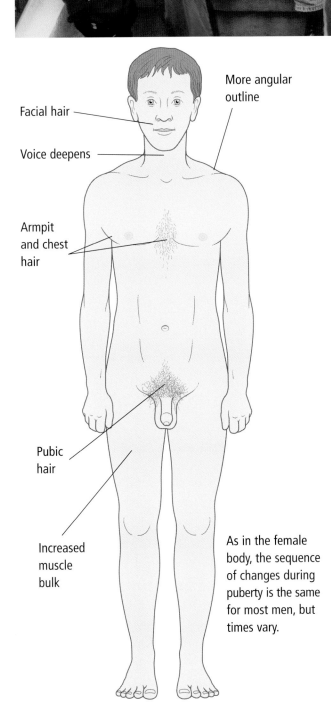

Facial hair

Voice deepens

Armpit and chest hair

Pubic hair

Increased muscle bulk

More angular outline

As in the female body, the sequence of changes during puberty is the same for most men, but times vary.

MALE CHANGES

On average, the male body grows faster than the female during puberty, so that it ends up slightly taller. The male body's outline also becomes more angular, with a greater proportion of muscle. Hair grows on the face, under the arms and around the penis and scrotum. The voice 'breaks' or 'cracks' and becomes much deeper because the voicebox in the throat grows rapidly at this time. The testes, penis and other reproductive parts enlarge and sperm production begins. Most of these changes are controlled by the hormone testosterone from the testes.

THE NEXT GENERATION

THE ABILITY TO REPRODUCE

The human body reaches adulthood and grows to its tallest height and greatest all-round physical ability at the age of 20–25 years. Its ability to reproduce usually begins before this, at puberty (see pages 42–43), and lasts for many years. In most women, from the age of about 50 years the female cycle gradually becomes less regular and then ceases. This time is known as the menopause. In men, sperm production begins to reduce slowly from the age of 30 years, but it may continue to 70 years old or more.

AGEING

In general, after 40 years old the body shows signs of ageing. Muscles become less powerful, bones slightly weaker, joints slightly stiffer, the heart and

Many people stay fit and active well into their later years – and at any age, a positive attitude helps enjoyment of life.

ANIMAL VERSUS HUMAN

In developed countries, most people live to 75–80 years of age, and some to more than 100. Yet certain animals live far longer. The rare lizard-like tuatara of New Zealand does not begin to breed until it is 25 years old, may still be reproducing when it reaches 100 and lives to perhaps 140!

In general, bigger animals live longer. But the tuatara, a reptile of New Zealand, has a very long reproductive cycle for its size. If it could grow as big as a human being, this might take more than 1,000 years!

lungs less efficient, the skin more wrinkled, the reactions slower, and the senses such as sight and hearing less keen. But the ageing process is so variable that in some people it is not noticed until 60 years old or later. Mental abilities such as learning may also become slightly slower. But experience shows that people who stay active mentally all through their lives, tend to have less mental deterioration as they become older.

HEALTH CHECKS

Regular medical checks are important all through life, but their details change with age, from baby to young adult to older person, according to the risks of ill health at each stage. In particular, many women are advised to attend for cervical screening. A tiny sample or 'smear' is taken from the cervix (neck of the uterus) and examined in the laboratory for changes which could indicate serious disease. Another check, especially for older women, is a mammogram, an X-ray photograph of the insides of the breasts.

THE REPRODUCTIVE CYCLE

The body's reproductive parts are not essential for the life of the body itself. Indeed, to treat certain diseases, one or more reproductive parts may be removed during an operation. However reproduction is essential for humankind to survive. We have a reproductive cycle, just like other forms of life – babies are born, who grow into youngsters, and become mature adults, who can have babies of their own.

GLOSSARY

abdomen The lower part of the main body or torso, below the chest, which contains mainly the parts for digestion, excretion and reproduction.

artery A blood vessel with thick, muscular walls that carries blood under high pressure away from the heart.

brain An incredibly complex part of the body, in the upper part of the head, made of billions of nerve cells and nerve fibres. The brain receives information from the senses, controls the body's movements, and is the site of thoughts, memories, conscious awareness and the mind.

cartilage A strong, tough, lightweight, fairly stiff but slightly bendy substance, that makes up structural parts of the body such as inside the nose and ears, and which also covers the ends of bones in most types of joints.

cell A single unit or 'building block' of life – the human body is made of billions of cells of many different kinds.

cervix The main opening or 'neck' of the uterus (womb).

cilia Microscopic hair-like parts that can waft or wave to and fro, such as those lining the nasal chambers inside the nose.

egg cells Small single cells made in the female reproductive parts, one of which joins with a sperm to begin development of a baby.

embryo The name for a developing human body during its earliest stages, to eight weeks after fertilization.

epithelium A layer covering the surface of a body part or forming its inner lining.

fertilization When an egg cell and sperm cell join to form the fertilized egg, which begins to develop into a new human body.

fetus The name for a developing human body during the later stages in the womb, from eight weeks after fertilization until birth.

follicle In the female reproductive system, a bag-like container of fluid and an egg cell, which enlarges as the egg cell becomes mature or ripe, ready to be released.

genes Instructions in the form of the chemical DNA, for how the body grows and develops and maintains itself.

hormones Natural body chemicals made by parts called endocrine glands, that circulate in blood and control many processes such as growth, the use of energy, water balance and the formation of urine.

immunity The ability of the body to recognize germs (harmful microbes) and destroy them before they can multiply and cause disease.

implantation When the tiny ball of cells which is the developing baby (embryo) burrows into the thickened lining of the uterus (womb) to continue its development.

IVF In vitro fertilization, a general name for bringing eggs and sperm together outside the human body so that fertilization can occur.

mammary glands Parts of the female body, within each breast, which make milk to feed the newborn baby.

mental Based in the brain or mind, and concerned with thinking and behaviour.

motor In the body, to do with movements or motions, such as motor nerves which carry motor nerve signals to the muscles to control their movements.

nerves Long, thin, string-like parts inside the body, which carry information in the form of nerve impulses or signals.

ovaries The two female reproductive parts that produce egg cells and also make hormones which control female development and the reproductive cycle.

ovulation Release of the mature or ripe egg cell from its bag-like container, the follicle, in the ovary.

oxygen A gas making up one-fifth of air, which has no colour, taste or smell, but which is vital for breaking down nutrients inside the body to obtain energy for life processes.

pelvic region The lower part of the abdomen, in the base of the main body or torso, where most of the female reproductive parts or some of the male ones are positioned.

pituitary gland A tiny part under the front of the brain inside the head, which makes many different hormones and controls various bodily processes such as growth and development.

placenta A plate-shaped reproductive part which develops in the lining of the uterus (womb), which passes oxygen and nutrients from the mother's blood system to the blood system of the developing baby.

pregnancy The time when a baby is growing and developing inside its mother's uterus (womb), before birth.

prenatal Before birth.

puberty The time when the body grows rapidly and the reproductive parts begin to function.

reflex A quick automatic reaction by the body, to a sudden change or situation which could be harmful, such as blinking the eyes if something comes near them.

skeleton All of the body's bones and also the supporting parts made of cartilage, or 'gristle'.

sperm cells Tiny single cells made in the male reproductive parts, one of which joins with an egg to begin development of a baby.

testes The two male reproductive parts that produce sperm cells and also make hormones which control male reproductive development.

urethra A tube leading from the urinary bladder to the outside, along which the waste liquid urine passes during urination.

uterus The female reproductive part in which the baby grows and develops before birth, also known as the womb.

vein A blood vessel with thin walls that carries blood under low pressure back to the heart.

FURTHER INFORMATION

BOOKS

The Reproductive System, Pam Walker, Elaine Wood, Charles Clark (Lucent Books, 2003)

Birth and Reproduction, Angela Royston (Heinemann Library, 1997)

Digestion and Reproduction, Andreu Llamas, Luis Rizo (illustrator) (Gareth Stevens Inc, 1998)

What's Happening to My Body? Book for Girls: A Growing Up Guide for Parents and Daughters, and *Book for Boys: A Growing Up Guide for Parents and Sons*, both by Lynda Madaras and contributors (Newmarket Press, 2004)

It's So Amazing! A Book About Eggs, Sperm, Birth, Babies, and Families, Robie H. Harris, Michael Emberley (illustrator) (Candlewick Press, 2002)

ORGANIZATIONS

National Childbirth Trust
The NCT offers support in pregnancy, childbirth and early parenthood.
Alexandra House, Oldham Terrace, Acton, London W3 6NH Tel: 0870 770 3236
Enquiry Line: 0870 444 8707

The Prostate Cancer Charity
Raises public awareness and provides information about services and support.
3 Angel Walk, London W6 9HX Tel: 020 8222 7622

Breast Cancer Campaign
Funds independent breast cancer research throughout the United Kingdom.
Clifton Centre, 110 Clifton Street, London EC2A 4HT Tel: 020 7749 3700

BLISS
The premature baby charity.
9 Holyrood Street,
London Bridge, London SE1 2EL
Tel: 020 7378 1122

Restricted Growth Association
Support for affected families and individuals.
PO Box 4008, Yeovil, BA20 9AW
Tel: 10 935 841 364

INDEX

afterbirth 27, 31
ageing 44–45
amnion 22, 24, 26

birth 30–31, 32–33, 34–35
birth canal 6, 7, 29, 30, 34
blastocyst 18, 19
breasts 28, 29, 32, 42, 45
breech birth 34

caesarian section 34
cervix 6, 7, 45, 46
  birth 29, 30, 34
  fertilization 17
  fetus 24
  menstrual cycle 9
  placenta 26
childhood 38–39, 40–41
chorion 22, 24, 26
chromosomes 18
conception 19, 20
corpus luteum 10, 11

egg cells 5, 46
  fertilization 16, 17, 18
  menstrual cycle 8, 9
  ovaries 6
  ovulation 10, 11
  reproductive problems 20, 21
ejaculation 16
embryo 22–23, 27, 46
endometrium 6, 9, 26
epididymis 12, 13, 14, 15, 16

fallopian tubes 6, 7
female reproductive system
  6–7, 21, 46
fertilization 16–17, 20, 22, 46
fertilized egg 5, 9, 16, 18–19, 21
fetus 24–25, 46
follicle 9, 10, 11, 46
FSH 9, 15

hormones 46, 47
  male 15
  menstrual cycle 9
  milk 32
  ovary 11
  pregnancy 27, 30

puberty 42, 43
  reproductive problems 21

immunity 39, 46
implantation 18, 19, 46
infancy 36–37
IVF 21, 46

male reproductive system
  12–13, 14
  problems 20, 21
mammary glands 29, 32, 46
menstrual cycle 8–9, 27 42
milk 32, 33, 37, 46
  pregnancy 28, 29

oestrogen 9, 11, 42
ovaries 6, 7, 46
  fertilization 17
  hormones 9
  menstrual cycle 8
  ovulation 10, 11
  puberty 42
  reproductive problems 20, 21
oviducts 6, 7, 11, 17, 18, 19
  reproductive problems 20, 21
ovulation 8, 9, 10–11, 46
  fertilization 17
  reproductive problems 20, 21
oxytocin 30, 32

penis 12, 13, 17, 43
period 8, 9, 27
pituitary gland 8, 9, 15, 30, 32,
  47
placenta 26, 27, 47
  birth 31, 32
  embryo 22, 23
  fetus 24
  hormones 30
pregnancy 5, 7, 19, 28, 47
  fetus 24
  hormones 30
  reproductive problems 20
premature birth 35
progesterone 9, 11
prostate gland 12, 13, 16, 17
puberty 42–43, 44, 47

scrotum 12, 43
seminal glands 12, 13, 17
sex 5, 13, 17, 20
sex organs,
  female 6
  male 12
sperm cells 5, 7, 46, 47
  fertilization 16, 17, 18
  production 14–15
  puberty 43
  reproductive problems 20
  testes 13
sperm ducts 12, 13, 14, 16

testes 12, 13, 16, 47
  puberty 42
  sperm production 14, 15
testosterone 15, 43
twins 17, 35

ultrasound scan 28, 29
umbilical cord 26, 27, 32
  birth 31
  embryo 22
  fetus 24
uterus 6, 7, 18, 19, 46, 47
  birth 31, 32, 34
  embryo 22
  fertilization 16, 17
  fetus 24, 25
  hormones 30
  menstrual cycle 8, 9
  placenta 27
  pregnancy 26–27, 28
  reproductive problems 21

vagina 6, 7
  birth 30
  fertilization 17
  fetus 24
  menstrual cycle 9
  puberty 42
vas deferens 12, 14
vernix 25

womb 6, 7, 46, 47
  embryo 23
  fetus 24
  pregnancy 21, 26–27